Gaki's Biblical Bedtime Stories

Apostle Rougaki Lee

Illustrated by Brittany N Deanes

Illustrated by Brittany N Deanes

Hardcover: ISBN: 978-1-960853-44-8

Liberation's Publishing - Columbus, MS

I would like to first and foremost thank my heavenly Father for the determination and the inspiration in guiding me while on the journey to writing Gaki's Biblical Bedtime Stories. I thank God for showing me how to compose and present the Biblical Bedtime Stories with artwork. Thank you, Brittany Deanes, for the vibrant and colorful artwork, you did an awesome job illustrating the artwork.

Composing and the completion of this book has been a blessing to me, and I pray it will be a blessing to you and your children and your children's children, and to all who read Gaki's Biblical Bedtime Stories. May God bless and keep you is my prayer.

-Apostle Rougaki Lee

In peace I will lie down and sleep, for you alone, O Lord, will keep me safe.

Psalm 4:8 NLT

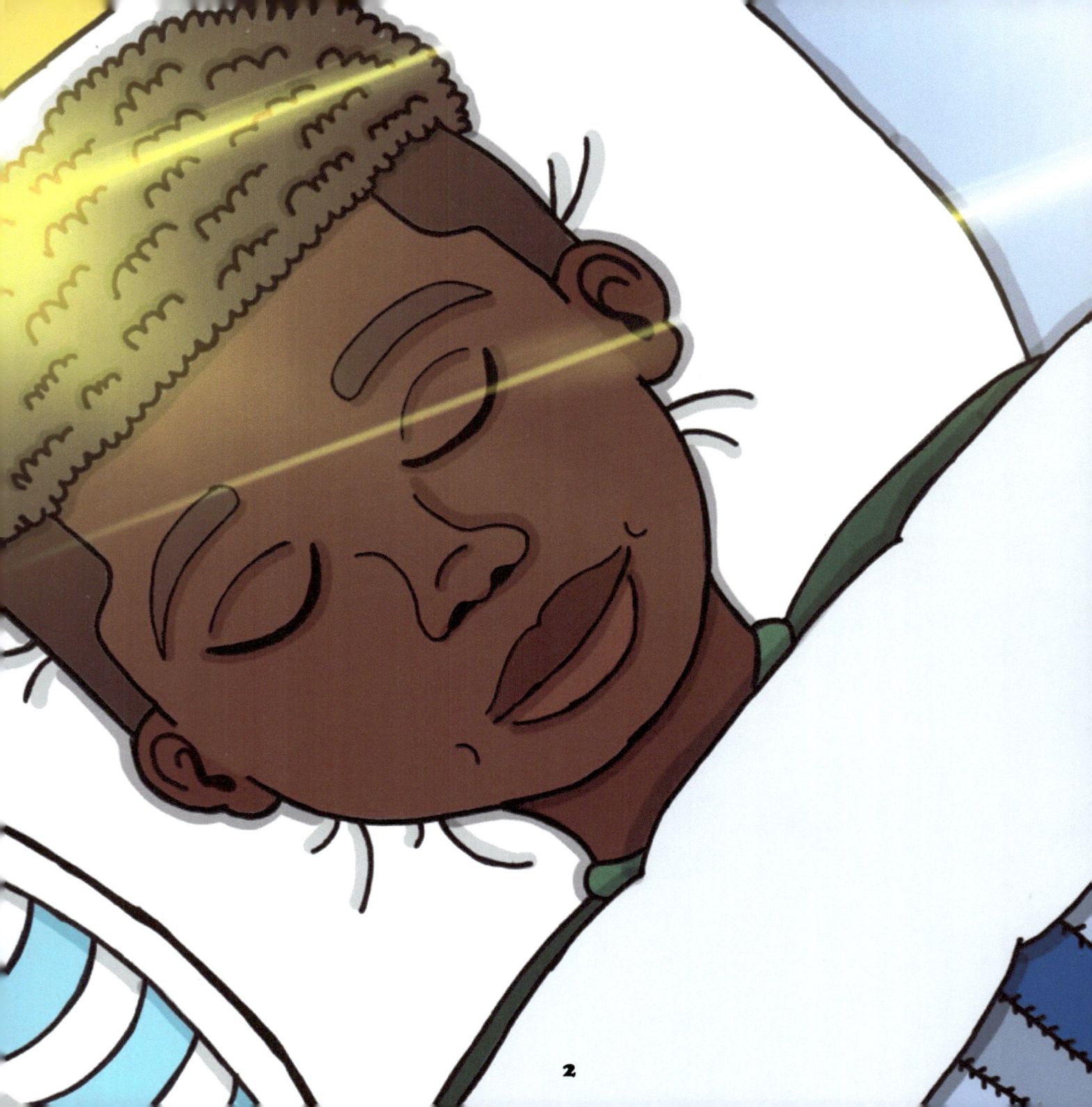

You can go to bed without fear; you will lie down and sleep soundly.

Proverbs 3:24 NLT

4

I am leaving you with a gift-peace of mind and heart. And the peace I give is a gift the world cannot give. So don't be troubled or afraid. John 14:27 NLT

The Lord is near to those who have a broken heart. Psalm 34:18 NKJV

Whenever I am afraid, I will trust in You.
Psalm 56:3 NKJV

Then Jesus said, Come to me all of you who are weary and carry heavy burdens and I will give you rest.

Matthew 11:28 NLT

Therefore do not worry about tomorrow, for tomorrow will worry about its own things. Matthew 6:34 NKJV

Thou wilt keep him in perfect peace, whose mind is stayed on thee: because he trusteth in thee. Isaiah 26:3 KJV

Casting all your care upon him; for He careth for you. 1 Peter 5:7 KJV

Those who live in the shelter of the Most High will find rest in the shadow of the Almighty. Psalm 91:1 NLT

This I declare about the Lord: He alone is my refuge, my place of safety; he is my God, and I trust him. Psalm 91:2 NLT

The Lord is my shepherd; I shall not want.
Psalm 23:1 KJV

24

He maketh me to lie down in green pastures: he leadeth me beside the still waters. Psalm 23:2 KJV

He restoreth my soul: he leadeth me in the paths of righteousness for his name's sake.
Psalm 23:3 KJV

Yea, though I walk through the valley of the shadow of death, I will fear no evil: for thou art with me, thy rod and thy staff they comfort me. Psalm 23:4 KJV

Prayers!

Now I lay me down to sleep

I pray the Lord my soul to keep

If I should die before I wake

I pray the Lord my soul to take

In Jesus name, I pray,

Amen

I will lift up mine eyes until the hills, from whence cometh my help. My help cometh from the Lord, which made heaven and earth

Psalm 121:1-2 KJV